NLP Productivity

Reach Success Using Neuro-Linguistic Programming Transformational Confidence Creator Life Habits 2.0: Goal Setting, Time Management, Morning Routine, Leadership and Increase Energy

Adam Hunter

Table of Contents

consent and can in no way be considered an endorsement from the trademark holder.

Introduction

Do you know what it means to have a productive mindset? A productive mindset means that you use your resources the best that you can. Your resources are your efforts, energy, and time. It means that you aren't trying to do everything or trying to do things the quickest way possible. It is making the best and most of the things you have while enjoying yourself. In order to do this, there are a few characteristics or qualities that can help you in accomplishing this.

These include:

- Curiosity – You are willing to explore, question, and seek out new concepts and ideas. You want to learn and understand more than you already do.

- Motivation or Desire – Without these things, you don't have anything to drive you to improve and progress. Inertia is what happens when you don't have the desire and it destroys progress.

- Vision – You are able to see what you want and this will give you focus and ideas of what you would like the outcome to be. Without this in mind, it would be hard to strive for your goal.

- Critical Thinking – Having the ability to assess different situations objectively or to see things how they really are. You are able to look at the pros and cons and you can make appropriate adjustments.

- Self-Confidence – Having the belief and faith that you are completely able and can do whatever you want. Without this, you won't be able to reach your full potential.

- Persistence – The majority of things won't come easily. You have to be willing to overcome adversity. You have to challenge yourself and persist so that you can reach your goals. Never let your circumstances, other's opinions, or setbacks keep you from reaching your goals.

- Positive Outlook – Your attitude, no matter negative or positive, will make or break you. Having a positive attitude will allow you to reach anything, but a negative mindset will defeat you before you get going.

- Open-Minded – An open mind allows you to create innovative new ideas. You will be open and receptive to new experiences.

- Balance – In order to function well, it's important that you remain balanced. It's important to work towards goals, but you have to take time to recharge and rejuvenate. Pushing yourself too much or trying to do too much will end up causing you to become frustrated and burned out.

By making sure that you follow the elements above in your life, you will create a productive mindset and set yourself up to reach your goals in a more effective manner, develop good habits, and improve your mind to function better. You have more time than you believe you have. You aren't busy. Actions will bring the results that you are looking for and your future self will thank you for it. NLP has the ability to help you with this.

It's amazing to find out how quickly you can learn how to switch up your habits when you want to. Eating, nail biting, smoking, and sleep habit can be changed using NLP. People who use NLP to change their lives are often skeptical about how quickly it can happen. Things can change in one session. In one case, a man was able to use a small NLP technique that took 25 seconds to break a 17-year-old nail biting habit.

People have been able to give up lifelong habits in a single session. NLP can give you the mental tools that you need to be successful in your life. One of the main things about NLP techniques is that you will step out of yourself and view yourself in the light that you want to as an observer.

This probably sounds very simple, and you could be saying "What's the big deal?" But when you actually do these things in a specific way, in a very deliberate way, you will be able to make a mental image so compelling that you attract it into your life. You will become a magnet getting pulled away from your old self and into your new self as the person who is no longer held down by their old habits.

You will become the person that you have always wanted to be. The reason NLP works so well is that you will be dissociated and you will see yourself in your mind in a compelling and new way. This process has a lot of magic and power. The key to NLP techniques is repetition, visualization, and imagination.

Since the unconscious mind is unaware of what is real and what isn't, a new habit has the ability to be created through mental repetition and rehearsal. In fact, a lot of professionals will use mental rehearsal to improve their work. Mental rehearsals can help you to change your habits without having to physically repeat it over and over again. In many NLP techniques, you will associate your new behavior with a specific trigger. This trigger could be a feeling or an object such as a telephone. When you repeatedly associate that trigger with your new habit, you will start to create a habitual response that will end up being triggered when the trigger is presented.

Importance of Habits

Habits are what makes or breaks success. Even though they are important, very few people know how to make habits work. A lot of people will associate the word habit with negative things like a drug or gambling habit. But the majority of habits are positive, like meditating, exercising, or starting a project long before it is due.

A habit is something that you do regularly without having to consciously decide to do it. It's an automatic behavior. Habits are what allow you to do things without having to use a bunch of mental effort. They are what make your everyday life possible.

There are a lot of people who try hard to break bad habits. Dieting is the big one. When a person chooses to follow a diet, they are trying to break the habit of overeating or eating bad foods. A lot of alcoholics and smokers want to break their habits, and there are just as many supporters out there who are willing to help them.

Over the last several decades, researchers have come to realize how important habits are. Here's a powerful story of the importance of habits. In 1993, Eugene Pauly was rushed to the hospital with a 105-degree temperature, vomiting, and stomach cramps. He was diagnosed with viral encephalitis. He was in a coma for ten days, and when he came to, his wife had to face the fact that he was no longer Eugene. He was still able to speak, but he didn't know the day of the week, could recall conversations, would cook breakfast but not eat it, fall asleep, and then fix the same meal a little while later.

A scan discovered that the virus had almost destroyed his medial temporal lobe, which controls recall functions and emotions. Eugene and his wife moved so that they were close to their daughter and one of the main and most important parts of his daily habits was walking around their block. Doctors had told his wife that Eugene needed to be under constant supervision. If he were to get lost, he wouldn't be able to make it back home. I mean, he couldn't even tell you what door in his house led to the kitchen.

His wife got up one morning and got dressed. When she went to find Eugene, he wasn't there. She ran out into the neighborhood screaming for him because even a person tried to help him, he wouldn't be able to tell them where he lived. The doctors have told her, in no uncertain terms, that he would never be able to find his way home. She went home not knowing what to do. Guess what she found?

Eugene was watching the history channel and a pile of pinecones laid on the table that he had collected on his walk. Repetition is what allowed him to do this. When you do something often enough, what is known as chunking will take place. The brain will change a series of conscious actions into something automatic that doesn't have to be thought about. Eugene formed a habit.

Mistakes

Starting a journey towards productivity is an amazing thing. The problem is that a lot of people will make mistakes that can be avoided. Let's look at the top five.

1. *Not having a clear vision*

People who are focused on being productive will start trying to do things better and faster and will end up forgetting the main point of what they are doing. Focusing too much on the 'how' will cause you to forget the 'why'. If what you are doing isn't meaningful, then why is it so important that you can do so much of it?

2. *Multitasking*

Everyone wants to get as much done as they can and multitasking may seem like a good idea but it won't help you. The human brain does better when you focus on a single task at a time. If you are reading something while talking to somebody else, you aren't going to retain much of the information. Multitasking ends up being counterproductive.

3. *Using too many tools and systems*

There are a lot of "productivity systems" out there and they can be tempting to buy all of them. Each one of them has a learning curve, so it's going to take time to learn every single one of them. This is counterproductive. Pick one system you like, learn it, and use it.

4. *Taking on too much*

Sure you want to get more done, but just because you are doing more things doesn't mean you are being productive. You won't be able to get everything done in the timeframe that you need to. This can also lead to burnout, which will slow you down even more.

5. *Not enough sleep*

When you try to be too productive by taking on harder and more projects, you have less time for yourself. This will cause your sleep to suffer. Nobody can function on only four hours of sleep. This is one of the biggest mistakes that anybody can make. Sleep is so important for a healthy mind and body and should never be sacrificed in the name of productivity.

With this in mind, let's look at how you can become productive in a good way.

What Do You Want?

A lot of people suffer from being too rational. They have big dreams they would like to achieve but they hold back by being too caught up in all the risks. They don't want to disrupt anything, and therefore, always play it safe.

In order to get themselves out of their comfort zone, they set goals. The process of making goals is like setting checkpoints along the road to a wanted outcome. Making and reaching little goals could serve as a way to check your progress. You can measure how far you have advanced and will show you how viable your plan is.

You need to approach setting goals just like you would a road trip. You need to create a roadmap and chart your success along the way. When you plan a long road trip, you know your destination, but because the trip is long, you need to make some stops along the way.

Before starting out, you decide you want to stop after a few hundred miles to get some food, then you will need to stop about halfway to refuel the car. Around the three-quarter mark, you decide to stop and stretch your legs and in another 100 miles, you need to stop to get more gas.

At every stop, you are meeting a small goal that will eventually get you to your final goal.

What can you do if you don't know what you want to do with your life? Not to worry, this is a problem for many people.

For some people, this isn't a problem at all. For others, it might take them a lifetime to figure it out.

It is easy to do the same thing day in and day out. It is familiar and comfortable. For people who want fulfillment in their lives, the following questions will help you see a clear picture of what you would like to do with your life:

1. What have I already accomplished in my life?

Think about all of your experiences and what you are the proudest of. Did these accomplishments make you feel good? Bad? Most of them probably made you feel good about yourself, right? Why not try to copy those feelings and experiences?

If you have ever signed up and finished a marathon, you probably felt very well about yourself afterward, didn't you? Why not begin training for another one? If you had children who grew up to be a musician because you taught them they could be whatever they wanted to be when they grew up, then you could be a mentor to other children.

Keep doing what makes you feel fulfilled.

2. If there were no limits on your life, what would you choose to do or have?

Try this: If you didn't have any limits, what would you do?

If time or money was no object, who would you spend time with? What would you love to do? Where in the world would you go?

Answering these questions could help you find out what you would like to do in life. This isn't saying you need millions to find happiness.

What it is saying is when you answer these questions, it will help you set goals, to reach milestones, and make a path to fulfillment and happiness.

Don't think about limitations and things that might be impossible, think about how much you want these things in life.

Remember, it is possible to start over and do things you really want to do.

3. What are you most passionate about?

When you want to have a very fulfilling life, you have to think about things that you are passionate about.

You absolutely have to know what you are passionate about so you can figure out what makes you happy and drives you. Ask yourself this:

What "jobs" have you done that don't feel like "jobs"? What makes you feel fulfilled? What things do you love? Do you like writing? Do you love being around animals? Do you like taking pictures of things?

The main point is, find out what you absolutely love to do and do more of it.

4. Are there any people in the world you admire?

If you follow the same path that successful people walked, you could have the same success.

Think about all the people you admire and respect. What qualities do they possess? Could you learn anything from them? What about them makes you respect them?

You are the average of the five people that you spend the most time with. Never waste time with people who tell you that you can't reach your dreams.

Spend as much time as possible with optimistic, successful, happy people and you might turn out just like them.

5. Do you have any goals in your life?

Goals are necessary if you want a happy future. Answer these questions:

- What goals do you have for your family?

- What goals do you have for your career?

- What goals do you have for your health?

When you have answered these, you will have a better idea of what you need to do in life.

6. *Are there things you don't like doing?*

One way to figure out what you would like to do with your life is to honestly assess the things you don't like to do.

What things do you absolutely despise? Are there things about your current job that you don't like?

You might not like meetings but you have to sit through hours of them each day. If this is happening, find a career where you could work alone more.

The main idea is if you want to change your life, you have to take action. This brings us to the last point.

7. *Are you willing to work hard to get what you want?*

Amazing accomplishments don't come easy. You will need to make a huge effort if you want great things out of life. This means you will have to put in more hours than normal people. Get outside your comfort zone and learn everything you can so you can achieve everything you want to achieve.

Here's the best part: most of the time the journey is more fulfilling than the actual goal. It is during these insignificant, little moments that you will find an "aha" moment that will help you answer this question:

"What exactly would you like to do with your life?"

To help you answer this question, you need to make a personalized map to arrive at your goal by making the following types of goals: stretch, immediate, and intermediate.

Stretch Goals

Begin by creating a long-term goal that might take several years to reach it. Figure this out first since this goal is going to influence your immediate and intermediate goals.

Stretch goals need to be huge. Some of these goals might be more specific than others. One very specific stretch goal might be buying a million dollar home. A vague goal might be wanting to be a producer of a television show. A very vague goal would be working in the fashion industry.

It is fine to leave room for some interpretation. Be as specific as you can and leave room for adjustment. When you create a stretch goal, you can work out the checkpoints on the way.

Immediate Goals

You need to make immediate goals that are small enough that you will be able to meet them within a week. These goals should be more like activities that could be done easily in one week.

Ask yourself this question: What do I have to do this week that will help me move along toward my goal? What little things could I do that will move me closer to that goal?

If you are a writer, one goal might be to write for 30 minutes every day. You might be looking for a career change and you found a book that is about the field you want to enter. You could make an immediate goal to read that book. Make sure these immediate goals are realistic. Being able to accomplish these immediate goals should feel like baby steps. They will help you with your overall growth and development along with setting you up to finish your intermediate goals.

Intermediate Goals

These goals are broader than your immediate goals and might have monthly or even yearly goal.

One intermediate goal could be to apply for a training program or apprenticeship. If your goal requires you to relocate, quitting a job, or enrolling in school, set a deadline for making one of these steps happen.

Meeting intermediate goals will help you move forward toward your goal. Reaching them might shove you out of your comfort zone but that is fine. Discomfort helps us grow and become the person we want to be.

Now that you have answered all the questions and know how to set goals, stop and take the first steps toward making your life better. Set your goals because you are going to need them later. You will be able to look back at these each day if you truly want to be successful.

NLP

Many people ask the question: What is NLP? Well, simply NLP is Neuro-Linguistic Programming. It is an approach that offers people tools and techniques that will help them deal with life's challenges and opportunities. It is a practical discipline that wants to bring results into the world.

So, basically, NLP is studying what works and the situations that they work in.

Let's break down NLP into individual words and learn more about it.

Neuro relates to the body's nervous system. The way our nervous system functions gets influenced by information that we take in through all our senses. If we can learn to take in information accurately, we will listen better and be more observant. If we can be more open to feelings of our own and others, our brains will receive better information to help us make the best decisions for us. We will, therefore, be able to communicate both unconsciously and consciously better.

Linguistic deals with language. When we are more aware and can understand words along with their structure and how they are spoken, their rhythm, voice tone, and speed, the information we get from this will help us make decisions and communicate unconsciously and consciously.

Programming is referring to habits. Everyone develops habits, some are useful, some aren't. NLP will teach us how we will be able to develop and use helpful habits and get rid of habits that aren't useful.

Creating Reality

One belief of NLP is everyone is responsible for building their own map of reality.

These maps get filtered by our nervous system, beliefs, experiences, and senses. Basically, most of the challenges we face are based on how we perceive the world and not the world itself. This is similar to confirmation bias, cognitive dissonance, worldview, and mental maps.

If we had the ability to improve how we take in and use the information that we get from our senses, then we will be able to improve our performance.

Adding Structure

We need to be aware of, listen to, and notice how and what people feel, hear, and see. Being able to understand our senses and how they affect others and ourselves will help us develop strategies that will guide our behaviors.

NLP is guiding and leading others and ourselves. It isn't about forcing, tricking, or telling. It's about figuring out what is constructive for everyone.

Keeping all that in mind, my definition of NLP is: "NLP explores how we act, communicate, and think. It is how we imitate and improve on performance in many different activities. We then transfer the things we've learned onto other people."

Benefits of NLP

- Helps you connect to your motivation, values, and purpose.

- Your life will be more fulfilled and successful.

- Your performance at work will improve. You might even begin building and starting your own company.

- You will have better relationships at home and work.

- You will develop better, healthy routines.

- You will overcome blocks and constantly learn new skills.

- You will enjoy your hero's journey in your life.

Needed Attributes

There aren't any special skills needed to begin exploring NLP. Having an attitude of tenderness, fierceness, playfulness, and curiosity are useful but not necessary. When you want to find results while learning about NLP, being honest, open, courageous, and ambitious helps a lot.

NLP History

NLP was created by John Grinder and Richard Bandler about 40 years ago. They worked and studied under Fritz Perls, Virginia Satir, and Milton Erickson. These are all very talented therapists and psychiatrists during their time. They decided to look at a different approach. They wanted to bring measurable changes instead of just creating another theory.

Grinder and Bandler wanted to find out what strategies great performers used, how they did it, and what they did. They created ways to model these strategies so other people could replicate the performance. This became the first model of NLP.

They constantly refined and tested their subjects. When other groups heard about the benefits, NLP began to spread across many aspects of businesses, sports, arts, coaching, and any human endeavors.

Robert Dilts is an early pioneer of NLP. He is still doing great work with entrepreneurs in Silicon Valley. His concepts about logic are useful for businesses and individuals. Every level is important along with the alignment between them. There is always one level that will be a "sweet spot" for every person or business's development. Take a look at this breakdown:

- Purpose

    o What do you want?

    o What things would you like to contribute to other people?

- Identity

    o Who are you?

- Beliefs and values

    o What are your beliefs about the world?

    o What are your beliefs about yourself?

    o What is important to you?

    o Why do you act the way you do?

- Capabilities

    o What do your strategies look like?

    o How do you come up with a plan?

    o What capabilities and skill do you possess?

- Behavior

    o What actions do you take?

    o What do you do?

- Environment

    o When and where do you do what you do?

How NLP Works

Has there ever been a time in your life when you wanted to change bad behavior and do something totally different just to realize you fell right back into your old habits?

If you have ever wondered why we repeat old habits constantly, it is because limiting behaviors and negative emotions are stronger than our conscious minds. Because patterns and habits get generated and stored by our unconscious minds, we have to make a change at the unconscious level.

If we could just say: "I'm giving that up right this minute", then we wouldn't need any therapists.

Beliefs and behaviors that are unwanted were learned and stored on an unconscious level. These don't serve us any longer so we need to change them. When you were younger, you might have learned not to like peanut butter because you had a sibling that was allergic to peanut butter. There wasn't ever any peanut butter in the house so you never knew what it tasted like. You grew up thinking peanut butter was gross or bad for you. This got stored at an unconscious level and now you still don't know what peanut butter tastes like. This is an automatic response that you can't change consciously. They can only be changed at an unconscious level.

This is true with beliefs. You might let a belief that was formed when you were young continue to hold you back now. Such as, "I never finish anything I start." This is just a belief. It isn't true and can be changed on an unconscious level to something that will empower your life.

Most of the time, people don't realize how and why they do things. This is where NLP comes into play. It will help you understand and see how you can change your behaviors and responses that no longer work for you to ones that will give you a fuller, richer life. This is your life, get out there and live it.

It Can Change Your Life

NLP could help you with your fears. This isn't just referring to phobias about creatures or insects. This is talking about fears like being afraid of other people or public speaking. NLP could be used to develop confidence by ingraining the belief that you are brave enough to stand in front of a crowd. It can encourage you by telling you that you matter in society and aren't just another face in the crowd. NLP can help you overcome depression or low self-esteem.

NLP could also help you achieve your goals. With NLP, you can find your weaknesses and reprogram your brain in a way that will empower you and overcome your weaknesses. Many athletes today are turning to NLP to improve their abilities so they will be able to excel in their field. They aren't just pushing their bodies but they are pushing their mental capacities to greater heights. Just think about what you might accomplish if you just set your mind to do something and then use these techniques to help you.

NLP could also help you with your personality. It can teach you how to understand others. It could help teach you how to understand the emotions and feelings of others. You should start treating others better and motivate them to reach for their goals. Others might begin to see a change in your personality and you might begin attracting more friends or people that just want to be around you just because you are giving off positive vibes. Some people might look to you as their role model. Keeping that in mind, you might actually begin "coaching" others. They might even thank you for helping them achieve their goals.

Increase Energy

It is amazing when we realize that our moods can affect our energy. Negative and gloomy moods can blend together to become a habitual attitude.

What is more impressive and possibly scary is the way our moods affect our energy levels. What we think about and dwell upon will determine if we are going to feel lethargic and tired or vital and alert.

Yes, you can feel tired after a long day at work. Most of the time, we feel tired because we "think" we feel tired.

Could this possibly be true? Could your emotional state and outlook truly affect the amount of energy you have daily? Is this just a theory?

With NLP, it is thought that personal experiences are more convincing than research. You need to test all things, including this. This can be done in just a few minutes.

Compare these scenarios to figure out how your mood can affect your energy levels. You need to do these instead of just reading about them.

Read the description of each scenario and then just stop and think about it for a few minutes. Then get rid of it by getting up and moving around.

Continue this with each scenario.

Scenario One

Take a few minutes to relax and be able to experience this:

"It is in the middle of winter. It is Monday morning.

It is gloomy, dark, rainy, and cold. You hear the traffic going by. You know you have a heavy workload facing you when you get to work because another co-worker is on vacation and you are covering for them this week.

You also have to attend a very boring, two-hour meeting as soon as you get to work. You check your mail and find your credit card bill. It's a lot higher than you thought it was going to be."

At this very moment, how do you feel?

How much energy do you feel you have right now? If this was happening to you, would you:

- Be ready to meet and take on your work challenges?

- Look at the world with a smile on your face?

- Be walking with a spring in your step?

- Be running up and down the step?

- Be bouncing around?

Probably not. Many people will feel drained, deflated, and low thinking about all this.

Now get up and move around. Get ready for the next one...

Scenario Two

This scenario is a bit different. It is the same day with everything exactly the same except for one thing...

"It is in the middle of winter. It is Monday morning.

It is gloomy, dark, rainy, and cold. You hear the traffic going by. You know you have a heavy workload facing you when you get to work because another co-worker is on vacation and you are covering for them this week.

You also have to attend a very boring, two-hour meeting as soon as you get to work. Right before you leave for work, you get some wonderful news...

- Someone that you have liked for a long time sends you a text and wants to meet sometime this week.

    o How will this affect your work?

    o How much energy do you have right now?

    o Do you feel light as a feather or heavy?

- You received a large amount of money. It isn't large enough that you are able to give up your job, but you will be able to do a lot with it...

    o What emotions are going through your mind right now?

    o Is this going to change your energy levels for work?

    o Did this make you smile?

- You just received a phone call saying that interview you went on last week and now your dream job is within reach. You get to begin this new chapter in four weeks...

    o Does this make you want to go to work?

    o Are you running around jumping for joy?

    o What is your energy level?

- Your partner has just called you from her doctor's appointment and told you that she is pregnant. You've been trying for a long time...

    o Will this affect your work performance?

    o What emotions are you feeling?

    o What kind of mood are you in?

How different is your mood from the bad news to the good news?

Have a Stimulating Day

Never have a nice day, have a stimulating day. The way we think and what we think about will affect your energy. Constantly being negative and gloomy will erode your optimism if you don't pay attention to the way you live each day.

Wait, there's more...

Being optimistic and cheerful is not easy if you only try to do it mentally. It isn't all about the mind. You have to manage the way you live your life daily so your activities and routines stimulate you physically and mentally.

The good news is this doesn't mean you have to wake up earlier and work out until you are totally exhausted before you even go to work.

Body Affects Mind

Most people feel completely exhausted from time to time. At times they may have a reason to feel that way like when you have been working hard, experiencing stress, or working out a lot.

Sometimes it is just living through an ordinary daily life with all its struggles and routines that cause physical and mental weariness.

We get into ruts and start focusing on what isn't going right in our lives or the bad things that could happen. This will affect the way we move, sit, and stand. We begin slumping over. We walk slower. Our faces aren't animated. Gravity feels as if it is pulling us down.

These physical and mental patterns become normal. Our attitude will change and we begin to think "this is the way I am now" and just place to blame on our genes or age. This bleak attitude will even come up with more evidence that supports it.

What Can We Do?

Many people say the only way to fix this is by changing your diet. True, at times, being tired could be due to a lack of vitamin C and B, potassium, or magnesium. I haven't found anybody who has gotten rid of this type of tiredness by taking supplements. You would be better off by eating a healthy diet and eating meals at regular intervals.

Other people will tell you that you need to exercise. This is another good idea but when you are already feeling exhausted, thinking about exercise just makes you feel more tired. The answer might be undemanding and simple: you need to get out of your rut a little bit at a time.

Change Routines

Think about the last time you took a vacation. It doesn't have to be a long vacation either. Just taking a few days to get away from it all, seeing different locations, people, food, finding fun things while away, not worrying about things will give you a boost of energy. Before you realize it, you are looking at life differently.

You will be looking at yourself and others differently.

This is the main reason why people get tempted to move their holiday destinations. It never works because we love routines and those routines will bring us back to our same old attitudes.

Being stuck in routines will quench your joy to live. Even changing up your routine a little bit could break the cycle of boredom.

Ten Percent New

Everyone deserves a routine that will make their lives run effectively so they can get things done more efficiently.

Those routines that never end and never change are not useful. You need to balance this out by offering yourself the ten percent new. This will challenge you to do something new each day for two weeks.

Some simple things you could do:

- Talk to new people

- Try new foods

- Dress differently

- Pick a new location to shop in

- Go out to eat in the middle of the week

- Change up the order you do things

- Drive to work using a different route

This list is potentially endless as you can add your own.

Basically, you just want to begin making small changes and stick with it for two whole weeks. Stand back and feel the difference.

You could keep a journal to keep track of what you do and what happens but this would be for people who are skeptical or like keeping journals. If you already keep a journal, by all means, keep track of this but if you don't, then you don't need to start just to keep track of what you are doing.

Just Ten Percent?

For many people, changing a lot of things won't work well. It will only create resistance. It won't be efficient and will only disrupt. It is hard to keep up the momentum.

You have to stick with little changes. This is why the ten percent difference is better than 90 percent. This introduces us to make small adjustments and this is enough to get you out of daily ruts. If you make a ten percent change each day or so, think about the difference this can make in a year's time.

Why are Focus, Energy, and Time Important?

Your focus, energy, and time aren't limitless. Each of them is going to run out at some time. We need to use them wisely to get the most out of these resources. This is why being organized and planning pay off.

Before You Start

If you don't begin a plan by being clear in these four areas, it will be completely wasted.

- Direction: Where do you see yourself in years to come?

- Make simple goals along the way to check your progress.

- Main focus areas that will lead to tasks you need to work on right now.

- Main areas to develop: what attributes and skills are needed to reach your end goals.

Main Elements

Being organized isn't all that hard. It does require some persistence, time, honesty, courage, and ambition. It could be a lifelong project so you need to begin soon.

The best approach for most people is to begin small. Choose something that attracts you and works on it until it has become a new habit. Now add on the next piece of the puzzle.

You have to figure out what works for you.

After some time, you will have built up some confidence and momentum. Now would be a good time to go back and begin with a new sheet of paper and figure out how you want to approach every day from scratch. Remember to use the elements you found that work for you.

1. Make Priorities

You can't manage your focus, energy, and time if you don't know what is important to you. This is why you need to use the discovery phase.

The next step would be to set three priorities for the next year. This would be broken down into three-month goals, monthly goals, weekly goals, and daily goals. This means that you will know what your main priorities are at the beginning of each day. You might need to change them due to events that happen in your life, but that would make it a conscious choice.

It is great to review these daily. When beginning to do this, it might seem theoretical but once you make it a habit, it will suddenly make complete sense.

2. Improve Focus and Energy

You can't make time so you need to find things that will improve your focus and energy. These could include when you eat, what you eat, hobbies, meditation, relaxing, rest, and exercise.

If it is important to you, include them in your daily routines. They will improve your effectiveness.

3. Daily Routines

Creating routines and beginning new tasks will take energy but maintaining them won't be as hard. The key is to create some routines that help to support you. Try to clarify your priorities, evening and morning questions, and mentally think about how you want your days to go. Whatever focus, relaxation, eating, and exercising routines work for you, you need to do them.

After you have established these habits, they won't take that much energy or time and gives you the freedom to use the majority of your focus, energy, and time on things that are important during that moment in time.

4. *Timeboxing and Hotspots*

Every hour isn't the same. There will be times during your day where you can handle hard tasks. There will be times where you can't. There are times during your day when you shouldn't be working at all. It is useful to figure out when you are most effective and make sure you use this time for things that are difficult, urgent, or important. If you have to take a meeting during a time when you aren't at your best, prepare an agenda and rehearse when you are your best.

It would be best if you could give the main tasks sufficient time. Starve less important tasks by not giving them a lot of time. What you can do within that time will be good enough.

5. *Stacking Questions*

Great questions will lead your emotions and thinking. These will also lead your behavior. You need to keep a list of questions to situations that you might find yourself in.

For example:

- What will you stop doing? Can you outsource or delegate?

- What will you accept? You might not want to but you have to.

- What will you maintain?

- What will you begin doing or do more of?

- Will it be worth doing this? Can you invest the energy or time to make a difference?

- Are you being productive or just being active?

- Do you have three priorities for the day?

- Do you have three priorities for the week?

- Do you have three priorities for the month?

- Do you have three priorities for the next year?

- Where are you going?

- Is there any way you can help?

- Do you have any suggestions?

6. *Begin, sometimes sprint, always finish*

You need to set beginning and finishing times. Start off fresh. If your start isn't what you thought it should be, it is fine to begin over. Sprinting can be very helpful. No matter what you need to finish and have a way to finish. Make sure you close any open loops.

7. *Designing an Environment*

It is important to have people around you that will keep you creative, energized, on track, and focused. Your work environment can have the same impact, from the pictures, the color of the walls, reminders around you, or if your space is neat could either push you forward or hold you back.

Placing affirmations around you so they catch your attention can also keep you on track.

When you can, pick the people you work with and the environment you work in.

Just Begin. It Will Be Worth It

When you begin trying to get organized, the challenge will look impossible. The demands on your attention and time are hard and you might begin to feel like you won't ever have the energy or time to begin. It is just one more project that is going to take your time.

This is why you have to begin simple. Begin by setting an intention to be productive today. Figure out three things that you want to get done.

If things change throughout the day, it will be fine if you decide to change them instead of them being drowned out by distractions.

When the day is over, review it and see how everything went. Learn from the lessons the day gave you. Let them go and you can begin fresh tomorrow.

The investment is going to be worth it.

Discovering Your Purpose

Why do you need a purpose for your life? Having a purpose will be a filter for your goals, behaviors, and actions. It will tell you when you are or aren't being productive.

Dilts' Neurological Levels

On the tip-top of this is purpose. This governs everything in life.

Underneath this is identity. This is your sense of being and exactly who you are. You can have multiple identities such as mother, sister, photographer, or writer.

Next comes beliefs and values. These are unspoken rules that govern your behaviors, actions, and decisions. These are the guides to help you make tough decisions. They also help you decide what you will and won't do in your life.

Next are capabilities. This is just a different way of saying ability or skills. This is where limitations get defined.

The last two levels are environment and behaviors. The environment is the things and events that happen around us. Behaviors are what we do.

One interesting fact about this model is it creates clear distinctions between purpose, identity, and action. If you do something that society thinks is bad (this is your behavior), won't make you a bad person (this is your identity). These are two completely separate levels. What you do daily (this is your behavior), what you have been trained to do (this is your capabilities), the roles that you play (this is your identities), and your purpose might all be a bit different.

Five Questions to Find Your Purpose

Now that we've covered all that, here are five questions you need to ask yourself in order to find your purpose:

1. If you had the choice to do whatever you want with your life without any consequence, constraints, or limitations, what would you choose?

2. Have there been any recurring themes that have shown up in your life?

3. Do you have any unique talents you can give to humanity and the world?

4. What would you be willing to risk your life to do?

5. When you die after you have accomplished all you've wanted to, what would the world remember about you?

Food

The next time you feel your energy is depleted, don't reach for another cup of coffee or a candy bar. Yes, sugar and caffeine might give you a spike in energy, but you will have a crash later that will make you feel more tired than you did before.

Try these ten foods that can boost your energy naturally and leave you feeling alert all day. They can elevate your mood and even make you more productive.

- *Eggs*

These beauties are rich in protein. In order to get the protein from eggs, you don't need to drink them as bodybuilder's do. The protein will give you a steady source of energy with lots of vitamin B. Yes, they are great for building muscle.

- *Blueberries*

These berries enhance mental agility and cognitive function. They aren't called a superfood for anything. They are full of antioxidants.

- *Whole grains*

Yes, they do contain carbs but the complex carbs release steady energy through the entire day.

- *Leafy greens*

They are iron-rich that will improve levels of concentration. You aren't going to get super strength like Popeye, but leafy greens such as spinach and kale are full of iron that will help you feel energized. Fatigue is the most common symptom of iron deficiency. Spinach is full of iron. Iron will promote the circulation of red blood cells and this will make you feel more alert and will improve your concentration.

- *Popcorn*

This yummy snack is high in carbs and fiber but if you don't smother it in butter, it is very low in calories. Popcorn is a great energy booster for children.

- *Greek yogurt*

Greek yogurt is full of protein and is a great alternative for regular yogurt. It has fewer carbs and lactose that add calories. Greek yogurt can help you feel fuller longer because its protein is slow acting.

- *Spicy herbs*

Spices can boost your metabolism and gives you a boost of energy. Peppers have a compound called capsaicin that increases the metabolism and helps with digestion. Certain types might improve cognitive function.

- *Salmon*

This fish is rich in Omega 3 fatty acids. These fatty acids can elevate moods and protects against depression. Salmon is full of these fatty acids.

- *Dark Chocolate*

This yummy food contains theobromine and caffeine. Both of these will boost your energy levels. If you eat in moderation, the sugar and caffeine will not give you an energy crash. The darker the chocolate, the less sugar and the more it will boost your energy.

- *Almonds*

These nuts are full of magnesium and vitamin E. They are a great snack for an energy boost. These nuts are the most nutrient rich. They have a lot of protein to help you keep your energy through the whole day.

Sleep

Sleeping well takes more than just going to bed at the right time. Try to follow these tips to give yourself a great chance to get quality, consistent sleep every night. If you think you are doing everything possible to try and sleep but you don't have the energy to do what you love to do, you might have other problems. Talk to your health care provider about what could be causing your sleep problems.

1. Set enough time aside for sleep. Sleep is as important to your health as exercise and diet, so be sure to set aside enough time for sleep. Plan the rest of your day around that. A good night's sleep means getting seven to eight hours every night for adults, nine to ten hours for teenagers, ten hours for elementary school children, and 11 to 12 hours for preschool children.

2. Create constant habits. Since we are creatures of habit, we are normally more successful when we follow a routine. It isn't any different with sleep. From the pre-bedtime routine to going to bed, to falling asleep, and waking each morning at the same time, you will find that being constant will make it easier to fall asleep.

3. Make a sleep environment that is comfortable. Be sure your bedroom is comfortable, quiet, and cool. The bed needs to be especially comfortable. You might need to experiment and make an investment but finding a very comfortable pillow and bed will be invaluable. You spend at least one-third of your life in bed. This makes it the main area that you don't want to skimp on comfort.

4. Before bed, turn it all off. It might be your phone, tablet, computer, or television. You need to give yourself some time to relax and unplug before going to bed. Your body needs to associate your bed with sleep. These devices will ramp up brain activity instead of slowing it down. Bright lights you get from these devices can suppress melatonin production and this makes it hard to fall asleep.

5. Use sleep technology. There are many different technologies out there that could help you sleep better. ResMed has a sleep sensor called S+ that has a bedside monitor, web app, smartphone app that will help you track and understand your sleep patterns. It will then create feedback and suggestions to help you improve your sleep.

Exercise

If you are feeling sleepy, tired, sluggish, you don't have the energy to get you through your chores. Don't try to sleep in and skip the extra cup of coffee, just head to the gym.

Exercise can help keep your body fit and boost your mood. Both of these can contribute to your well-being and health. Exercise can boost several areas of wellness because it:

- *Increases endorphin levels*

Endorphins are a natural hormone in our body that gets released when we do something that requires us to use energy. They make us move. Exercise will increase these levels. It is the release of endorphins that give joggers the feeling of euphoria that many people call "runner's high".

- *Keeps your heart healthy*

Exercise can give your cardiovascular health a boost. This allows you to have more energy throughout your day. When you can do all your daily chores, you will have energy left over and won't feel as tired when all the work gets finished. For better cardiovascular health, it is recommended that you get about 30 minutes of aerobic exercise five days every week. If you want to lower blood pressure and cholesterol, try to get about 40 minutes of moderate to vigorous intensity aerobic exercise three to four times each week.

- *Will improve sleep*

Exercise lets you sleep better. When you get enough sleep, you will feel refreshed throughout your day. One study that was done on people who had insomnia had them engage in about 150 minutes of moderate intensity exercise in one week. They realized that this amount of exercise gave the volunteers a reduction in their insomnia. It also gave them a boost in their mood, too.

- *Will sharpen your focus*

Mentally, anyone will feel ready to tackle the world and energized after exercising because endorphins will boost our energy levels. Doing 24 weeks of moderate aerobic exercise can improve cognitive function like concentration. Some researchers say that high-intensity workouts won't have the same effects. Just one session of high-intensity training can improve cognitive function with respect to short-term memory tasks and attention.

What Exercise Will Give You an Energy Boost?

Any physical activity that will get your heart rate and blood going will release endorphins and this will raise your energy level. Good exercises that target the cardiovascular system will give you stamina and strengthens the heart.

An aerobic exercise is the best in helping depression symptoms. Low-intensity exercise like yoga has many benefits for your mood. Yoga can reduce anxiety and depression. Any physical activity or routine exercise can lower depression levels.

What exercises are best? That is completely up to you and the things you like to do. If you don't like doing it, it isn't going to do you any good. It needs to be something that is enjoyable. Pick things you enjoy doing like tennis, football, or basketball. Go for a bike ride in the park. Go for a walk or jog with friends. Take time for yourself and dance to your favorite music. Try a spin class, martial arts, or kickboxing.

The key is finding something that you enjoy so you will stick with it and you will soon be reaping the benefits of a regular exercise routine.

Self-Discipline

The human language can be a funny thing at times. Knowing the way our brains hear things is really very important. Take the concept of self-discipline versus being disciplined. They mean the same thing, don't they? Do they?

Being disciplined might mean you are disciplining yourself. You discipline yourself when you go to the gym every day. You discipline yourself when you hold back and don't argue. You discipline yourself when you save money rather than spend it.

What exactly is your mind hearing? Is it hearing that you are being disciplined or is it hearing you are getting punished? If somebody else disciplines you, it is punishment, isn't it? You have done something wrong so now you are getting disciplined. Is this what your mind is hearing? If so, it isn't any wonder we have problems keeping our promises.

Self-discipline means being deeply committed and focusing on what you want versus what you are wanting right now. This sounds like a choice, right? Since the word begins with "self", it is like you have made the choice of being disciplined instead of somebody else forcing us to do it.

Is there a simple definition of self-discipline? I would say that self-discipline is the art of making sure you take constant action that is in line with whatever your highest standards are. Whatever you want to do regularly in order to reach your future goal or the process of doing these things regularly is self-discipline. Is there a way to improve self-discipline? Here are some critical steps:

- You have to know what you want to do. This may sound like common sense, but you have to know what behaviors or activities you need to do and when you need to do them.

- You have to take time to realize the best way to get better at discipline is practicing it. The good part is you can practice on anything. It doesn't matter how small or large. Practicing anything regularly will improve your discipline. If it is just adding an apple into your daily routine, then you have to make sure you do it.

- Whatever you decide to do on a regular basis, you have to start at a set time and no matter how bad or good you did, you have to continue doing it at that specified time. Create your schedule around it. You need to make it a priority. You have to hold this priority sacred. Remind yourself why you do it. If you are beginning a jogging regimen, the benefits will speak for themselves. If you want to quit smoking, then the health benefits are obvious. Just figure out a time and remind yourself why you are doing it.

- This might be the hardest, but the most valuable secret that will help you deal with discipline. This part involves keeping up with the discipline. Many have experienced when we start to do something then we get tempted to stop right after starting. Here are some ways to overcome these temptations:

  o Allow yourself to see your projected future from two basic steps. Remember, it will be easier to do the discipline tomorrow if you do it every day. It will get easier with time. Imagine the rewards of continuing and ask yourself if it will be worth it.

  o Discipline helps build character and will make you a better person. Successful people are successful because they do what they like to do and they do things they don't like to do because they know it will let them have more of what they want.

  o Begin holding your valuable and sacred word inside you. We know how frustrating it can be when somebody tells you they are going to do something then they don't. Hold yourself to higher standards.

When you tell someone you are going to do something, be sure that you do it.

Reward Yourself

You need to reward yourself when you finish a task. Why should you do that? When you reward yourself, your brain sends out positive emotions that lead to realizing your efforts that will result in positive rewards. When you do this constantly, your brain will begin to link pleasure with accomplishing goals and moving you toward your future goals. You build upon success.

When you have finished your day, write down three accomplishments. It doesn't matter how small or big. Once you have achieved a goal, celebrate. Even small rewards will be a big motivator. It might be a coffee break, a walk in the park, or a mini vacation. When you reward yourself for all your victories both little and big, it will make a huge difference.

Psychology Behind Rewards

There are many ways you can change your habits. The best one is by giving yourself a reward.

Rewards might sound a bit self-indulgent or frivolous but it isn't. Since forming better habits might be draining, rewards play a major role. When you reward yourself, you will feel contented, cared for, and energized. This, in turn, will boost our self-esteem and this will help us keep up our good habits.

Studies have shown that people who reward themselves by buying themselves a gift or watching their favorite movie gained more self-control. This is a big secret about adulthood: When you give more to yourself, you can ask more of yourself. Self-regard is not selfish.

If you don't get any rewards, you will start to feel resentful, depleted, and burned out.

While talking with a friend about giving myself rewards when I accomplished a goal, they thought it was very strange that I rewarded myself for things I should have been doing anyway. They told me that they never give themselves rewards. This made me stop and think.

First off, it didn't matter if they gave themselves rewards or if they thought they were someone who didn't give themselves rewards. When talking about habits, it seems a bit risky.

This might seem selfless or even stoic to not give yourself rewards. When people don't get rewards, they will begin to feel deprived. Feeling deprived is a bad frame of mind to keep healthy habits. When people feel deprived, they begin to feel pressured to get themselves back into balance. If you can tell yourself that you have earned a reward, that you need and deserve it, you will feel tempted to stop your good habits.

Second, I began to think that he probably gave himself rewards, he just didn't think about them as rewards. After talking for a few minutes, he did tell me that he rewards himself because each week he purchases himself new music.

In order for something to be a reward, we have to think about it as a reward. We make it a reward when we call it a reward. Once we realize it gives up pleasure, it will become a better reward. Even something as simple as a cup of tea or a book of poems could be a reward.

When I realized that I love scented candles, a whole new world of rewards was shown to me.

Everyone needs to strive to have a large variety of healthy rewards so we can recharge our batteries in healthy ways. At times, rewards won't look like a reward. To my horror, many people think that ironing is a reward. Whatever you like, use it as a reward when you hit a goal in life.

Habits

It would be great if we could push an autopilot button and our lives would just take care of itself. We wouldn't have to worry about doing our work, eating right, exercising, or chores. They would just automatically be done. Unless technology invents robots that will do all that stuff for us, our work won't disappear overnight. If we could program our behaviors as habits, it could ease some of the struggles.

With a little bit of discipline, you can create new habits that require little to no effort to keep. Here are a few tips to help you create new habits and stick with them:

1. *Commit to 30 days*

This is all the time you need in order to get a habit to stick. If you can get through this phase, it will be easier to maintain. One month is a great time block to commit to changing because it fits easily into a calendar.

2. *Do it daily*

Consistency is critical to making habits stick. If you would like to begin exercising, go to the gym each day for 30 days. If you just go a few times each week, it will make the habit harder to create. What you do every once in a while is harder to turn into habits.

3. *Begin simple*

You can't change your life in one day. It's easy to over motivate yourself and try to do too much. If you want to begin studying for two hours each day, begin with a habit of 30 minutes and expand it every week.

4. *Keep reminders*

About two weeks into forming your habits is the forgetful stage. Put reminders up to help you remember your habit every day or you might forget for a few days. If you miss out on days, it will defeat the purpose of creating habits.

5. Be consistent

The more constant you are with your habit, the easier it will stick. If you want to exercise more, go to the gym every day at the exact same time for one month. When you add in cues like time of day and where, the circumstances remain the same and will be easier to stick with.

6. Find a friend

Find somebody who will go with you and keep you motivated when you feel like you want to quit.

7. Create a trigger

Triggers are rituals that you use just before doing your habit. If you want to get up earlier, this means waking up at exactly the same time every day. If you want to stop smoking, you might wear an elastic band around your wrist and snap it each time you feel the urge to smoke.

8. Replace any lost needs

If you are giving up something to form a habit, be sure you replace it with needs you are losing. If you watch television to relax, try listening to music, reading, or meditating to replace this need.

9. Don't be perfect

Your attempts to create or change a habit will not be successful. It might take you four tries to begin an exercise routine. Then one day, you just do it without realizing it. Try your best, but expect to have some bumps along the way.

10. Use the word "but"

If you begin to think negative thoughts, use the word "but" to interrupt your thought process. Like if you were thinking: "I am not good at this, but, if I keep practicing, I might get better."

11. Get rid of temptation

Change up your environment so you won't be tempted in your first 30 days. Get rid of all junk foods, cancel your cable, throw away all cigarettes so you don't have to struggle with your willpower later on.

12. Pick a role model

Spend time around people who have the habits you are trying to create. Studies have shown that if you are around skinny people, you are more likely to be skinny too. You basically become what you are around the most.

13. Do an experiment

Don't judge yourself until a month has gone by, just use this time as an experiment in your behavior. Experiments can't fail. They will just have different results. This gives you an alternate perspective when changing habits.

14. Swish

Think about yourself doing this bad habit. Now see yourself pushing that bad habit to the side and doing the opposite. End the sequence seeing yourself in a positive light. Watch yourself pick up a cigarette, see yourself put down that nasty cigarette and snapping the elastic band around your wrist. Last, see yourself running without any shortness of breath. Do this a couple of times until you get through the pattern before doing the bad habit.

15. Write it down

Having a piece of paper with a resolution on it isn't important. Writing that resolution down is. When you write, you make your ideas clearer and causes you to focus on your end results.

16. Know benefits

Get familiar with the benefits of making a change. Find materials that will show you all the benefits of eating healthier, exercising regularly, or quitting smoking. Watch out for any changes to your energy levels once you begin any of your new changes. Imagine what it will be like at the end of 30 days.

17. Know pain

You have to know the consequences. Find realistic information about the downside of not making new habits and this will give you more motivation.

18. Do it for you

Don't think about all the things you "should" do as habits. Move your habits toward your goals and what motivates you. Empty resolutions and weak guilt aren't enough.

Hacks

When you take a moment to look at your life as it is right now, what are some of the reasons you aren't healthy, happy, or successful?

Not counting the numerous excuses, there is probably one simple reason: no self-discipline. You just don't want to do what you have to do in order to have success. If you think about it, what is it going to take for you to be successful? It isn't a secret. Everyone knows what you need to do to live healthier. Everybody knows what they need to do to perform better at their jobs, but they won't do it. Everybody knows what foods to stay away from and what ones to eat, they still won't do it.

Knowing what you should do and doing it are two different things. If you don't have self-discipline, things won't ever get done.

Having success comes from the actions you take constantly. Having self-discipline lets you do that.

Here are five ways to build self-discipline:

1. Think long-term

This quote from Abraham Lincoln is a favorite of mine: "The best way to predict the future is to create it". If you ever think about where you are going to be in ten years, look at your life now. Are you taking any actions to turn your goals into reality? Are you reading any books to better yourself as a person? How many new things have you learned lately? Who are you associating with? Are you doing everything possible to achieve your daily goals?

People think their lives are going to change through some magical event but this isn't true. Your life will only change to what you are willing to change. If you aren't happy right now, what are you doing to change them? If you aren't, you are only daydreaming. Nothing is going to change if you don't change a little bit each day. To quote Aristotle: "We are what we repeatedly do. Excellence then is not an act, but a habit."

2. The enemy of success

The enemy of success is taking the path of least resistance. If you pick everything that is easy and fun over what is necessary, you won't ever reach the happiness and success you are seeking. This is because each victory requires some sort of sacrifice. If being successful was easy, everyone would be successful. Since success in all areas of life takes sacrifices and hard work, many people won't ever reach their potential.

When you decide to not do something you know you should do, you are wasting an opportunity to grow. You are also losing confidence in yourself. You begin to look at yourself as a lazy person. You think you will never be successful. And this self-image will become a prophecy.

3. Know in advance that you won't ever give up

In order for you to stay strong when facing adversity, make sure you have decided in advance how you are going to respond if it happens. You have to know what you are going to do when all hell breaks loose or you will just give up. When you write out your goals, no matter how hard they are, you have to commit to making them come true. Figure out who you are going to respond when faced with setbacks and failures so you can come back better and stronger.

If you can make this commitment and don't ever break it, you will be a success at everything you set your mind to. It might not happen immediately but it will eventually happen.

4. *Write your goals daily*

To keep yourself discipline daily, you have to keep the big picture in mind. When you remember why you do the things you do, you will take all needed actions to get it done. You don't work hard just because you want to. You have goals you want to reach and that makes the effort worth it.

To quote Nietzsche: "He who has a 'why' to live for, can bear almost any 'how'." This is so true. If you know deep down what you would like to do and have the reasons to do them, you will do what it takes.

The big problem is we get caught up in working and reaching our goals that we forget why we began this race. We forgot why we do the things we do and get caught up in the unending to-do list. This is why many people aren't excited about life. They don't have any goals to reach.

The easiest way to fix this problem is to rewrite your goals each day and see the future the way you want it to be. Each morning after you wake up, write down the goals you have in life. This will get you motivated immediately and it will excite you to begin your day. You have to be extremely clear on what you have to do in order to succeed. After you have focused on your goals and what you want out of life, you will be able to know what you have to do to make those goals happen.

5. Obstacles will happen

Nothing that is worth having will come easy in life. You will have to make sacrifices from time to time. They might be in the form of hard work, pain, effort, and time. You will have setbacks, and when you get close to succeeding, there will be another test to see if you really want it. After passing countless tests, will you finally succeed? The biggest tragedy in life is many people give up just before they finally succeed.

To grow as a person, you have to face life's challenges to succeed. It doesn't matter how long it will take or how hard it will get, remember these words of Les Brown: "It isn't over until I win."

Mistakes

Here are the most common mistakes that will ruin your self-discipline. Prevention is better than a cure and it isn't any different when you want to build your self-control.

1. Rely on willpower

The first mistake people make is they rely on willpower rather than planning for temptations. Don't rely on willpower alone, plan for any and all temptations and place roadblocks in front of them. If you are trying to diet, don't keep unhealthy foods in your house. Throw it away or give it away so you don't have to deal with the temptation.

2. False hope

The second mistake is a syndrome called false hope. This is where you have unrealistic expectations about the consequences, ease, amount, and speed of the changes you are going to make in life. People who have problems with this syndrome will try changing themselves just to fail every time since they have set an impossible goal.

It doesn't matter how self-disciplined you are, if your expectations are unrealistic, you are going to fail. It is important to know about this phenomenon and research what goals you can achieve realistically. If you go step by step instead of reaching for the moon immediately, you will save yourself a lot of anguish.

3. Underestimating stress

The third mistake is underestimating how much of an impact stress will have. Stress can affect the amount of self-control you have. If you don't take care of your mental health, your self-discipline is going to deteriorate. To keep this from happening, introduce some habits that will reduce stress in your life. Spend 30 minutes daily doing activities that relax you. Listen to music, meet with friends, read a book, cuddle with your pet, exercise, meditate, or take a walk.

4. Neglecting the sustainability of change

The fourth mistake is neglecting how sustainable your changes are. You may be tempted to introduce a lot of changes in your life and want them to stay around forever. Even self-disciplined people need to take breaks every now and then. If you don't think about how sustainable your resolutions are, you won't be able to develop good self-discipline. To stay away from this mistake, give yourself some leeway. If you would like to lose some weight, schedule some cheat days every now and then to give yourself a break.

5. Waiting for the perfect time

The fifth mistake is trying to wait for the perfect conditions. If you keep saying I'll start tomorrow, next week, next month, next year, 99 percent of the time, you will fail. There isn't any amount of self-discipline that will help you begin a diet, start a business, learn new skills, be a better wife and mother, begin saving money or find a dream job. Begin right away or realize you don't desire your goals enough.

Goal Setting

Probably one of the most important things you can do in reaching your dreams is creating your goals. You know what you want in life, but how are you going to reach it? That's where SMART goals come in.

But, before we look at how to create your goals, let's clear up any confusion between short and long-term goals. Beyond the obvious, understanding the difference between these two things can help you to navigate your path from the present to the future with shown progress. When you work towards specifics, it helps you to bring your vision to life.

Long-term goals tend to be strategic. This is the reason why they shape the direction of your life. The success of achieving these goals is a reflection of how well you have done overall. Short-term goals show how you are doing in a specific moment in life.

Short and long-term goals have the purpose of helping you to reach your overall desire in life, whatever that may be.

Short-term goals are typically goals that you can achieve in less than five years, and more likely within one to three years. They are made up of operational components that will affect your immediate future. They also help to create the action plan for reaching your long-term goals.

Long-term goals will take more than five years to achieve, and likely upwards of 10 or more. These are the big items in life that you want to reach, such as buying a million dollar house or having your company reach a worth of a million dollars. The short-term goals you decide on will help you to reach those long-term goals. Both long and short-term goals can be planned out using the following SMART method.

SMART goals stand for Specific, Measurable, Attainable, Realistic, and Time-lined.

Goal setting is very much a prerequisite to success in almost every part of your life, but 95% of people don't set goals. SMART goals coupled with NLP helps you to go past just setting a goal and to program your mind to drive you towards your goal. First, you will create your SMART goal.

Specific – You want to bring specificity into your goal so that you can find clarity by defining what exactly your core values are. If you create a goal that is too general, it will cause challenges when it comes to creating a workable plan. Saying I want to drop 30 pounds is better than I want to lose weight.

Measurable – Measurement is what can tell you how you are progressing. The way you measure your goals should align with what motivates you the most. For example, experiencing a happier mood and more energy may be a more motivating way to measure weight loss than looking at a number on the scale.

Attainable – Most likely your goal is going to be attainable. This just means that you will actually be able to achieve your goal. Everything is attainable; just make sure that with your time and resources that you will actually be able to reach that goal.

Realistic – While everything may be attainable, not everything is realistic. You can have a goal for becoming a millionaire, but if you add a timeline of one month, that's probably not that realistic. This type of goal is setting you up for disappointment.

Time-lined – This means that you have things mapped out in a time-based manner so that you have milestones and the like to help push you along.

Now is the time to pull in the NLP. This is where you will use a WISE approach to your goals.

What

If...?

State in positive

Envision

First is the "What If...?" part. Goal setting should be creative. What ifs can cause a catastrophe if there is an attachment of anxiety to the future. However, in this case, it can lead to enlightenment to what's possible as well as the possible speed bumps you might face.

What if I achieve my goal? What if I don't achieve my goal? What if I knew I would reach my goal?

These questions will provide you with "ecology," as it is referred to in the NLP world. Basically, it means you connect with the impacts and consequences to improve your alignment with your goals.

State in positive – It's important that you word your outcomes in the positive when setting goals. This means you use words that reflect what you want instead of what you don't want.

The power of wanting something is powerful. Think about when you told yourself, "I don't want to forget to grab flour at the store." You forgot to get it, didn't you? Next time, try saying "I must remember to get flour at the store." This mindfulness in wording is what stands between you are and your goals.

Envision – This is the fun part of goal setting. You get to think about what your life could be like once you reach your goals. Making sure that all your senses get used, ask yours: When I reach my goal:

- What tastes, smells, sounds, and sights surround me? How am I going to feel?

- Who will be with me? What will they say or do?

- What do I look like? What will I say or do? What am I wearing?

- Where will I be? What is it going to look like?

NLP refers to this practice as evidence. By using SMART and WISE goals, you will be able to achieve whatever you want in life. But the important thing to remember is that you actually write down your goals by hand. One study performed on goal setting found that those who wrote down their goals by hand were more likely to achieve them. They took a group of graduating college students and asked them to set goals. Some of the group didn't set any goals, others did but didn't write them down, and then a small percentage wrote down their goals. After several years, they interviewed the same students. The students who created goals but didn't write them down made twice as much as the students who didn't set goals, but the ones who wrote down their goals made ten times as much as the ones who didn't.

Most people think just having a goal in mind is enough, but it's not. The secret to reaching your goals involves writing them down in a clear and well-defined manner.

Written goals create a reminder. You can look back at the goals every day, or whenever, to remind yourself of what you want to achieve. Humans forget a lot of good ideas. They can vanish as quickly as they come. That's why writing things down is so important. You can't forget it if it's on paper.

It's also one step into bringing your vision into reality. Writing them causes you to commit to achieving them. When they are written, people don't feel the need to work towards them.

It can also help you to track your progress. We already talked about the importance of tracking your progress. You also need to track failures, that way you don't end up repeating mistakes. When you track yourself, you will find that you are more motivated to try harder.

Lastly, written goals help you to filter opportunities. As you start to achieve success in your life, you will notice more opportunities. These opportunities can be distractions that knock you off track. To fix this problem, you have to evaluate your list of written goals on a regular basis. This will help you to identify the things that will take you off track.

Breaking Down Goals

You should now have a good understanding of how to create long and short-term goals, but right now, I want to look at why it is so important that you break down your bigger goals into actionable steps.

The first thing, when setting your goals, should be to create your long-term goals. Once you have created your long-term goals that are obtainable and have a timeline, you can move onto medium-term goals.

This is your first stepping stone to achieving your long-term goals. This should be things that you can achieve in a little less time than it would take to reach your long-term goals. They also need to be specific and have a timeline.

Lastly, you will create the small-term goals. These are the actionable steps that you can take to reach your goals. These little goals are meant to make the large goal not seem so daunting. Because, if you think that you can't reach your dreams, then you won't. Then there comes a point where you have to start planning and start doing.

- Plan and prioritize your tasks to help you decide on what is the most important.

- The first step should only take 30 minutes. If it takes longer, try to break it down so that you are less likely to procrastinate.

- Every evening, reflect on tomorrow. Pick the tasks you want to work on.

- Come up with a to-do list to improve your focus, help you feel accomplished, and reduce stress.

- Write your three most important tasks down. Start with the first and work early in the day so that you have the most willpower.

- Be realistic about what you can accomplish in a given timeframe.

Doing this and accomplishing your smaller goals will keep you motivated. It will also help you to move closer to your long-term goals.

Mistakes

People tend to make mistakes when they set goals. It doesn't mean they are bad at it, mistakes just happen sometimes. There are five main mistakes that can create problems when it comes to setting and achieving goals.

1. *The goals are too big*

A common mistake people make with their goals is creating a goal that is too big. That doesn't mean you can't achieve it, but goals work best when they are doable with where you are in life right now. It's going to be very hard to start doing something that is in complete opposition to what you are currently doing. That's why you want to create actionable and concise goals so that they are easier to achieve.

2. *Setting too many goals*

Some people will get caught up in creating goals and can create too many to the point where they are overwhelmed. This will keep them from achieving any goals because they won't know where to begin. A couple of long-term goals broken down into actionable steps that you can take every day is the best way to improve your odds of reaching your goals.

3. *Focusing on outer attainment*

When you look over your goals, how do you feel? Do they make you feel excited or do you feel dread? Goals are only reached when you focus on how you want to feel once they are achieved. You can't successfully reach goals for somebody else. You have to reach them for you. You need to ask yourself why you want to achieve your goals.

4. Thinking it relies only on willpower

When your goals are exciting and motivating, you will start to give yourself a pep talk in order to achieve them. But the environment you have around your goals is also important, just as much so as willpower. Willpower isn't the only thing that you need to achieve your goals. There are ways to create an environment that won't require as much willpower on your part, such as shutting off electronics so that you won't be distracted.

5. Waiting until...

Many people will say, "I will get started working on that on..." They think there is a better time than now to start working towards their goals. The best time to start working on your goals is now.

Time Management

Have you ever had the feeling that time was just flying by, or that it was creeping along? Are there times where you feel overworked with too much to do and not the time to do it, or you are bored to tears and can hear the clock tick every second? If yes, then you probably struggle with time management.

You are among the many who wish that a day held 48 hours because 24 aren't enough. But through the power of NLP, you would find that 24 hours is just enough.

How do you manage time?

When it comes to NLP and time management, there are two main types of people: those who work "through-time" and those who work "in-time." People who work in-time don't notice the passage of time. They live in that particular moment and they don't worry about a timeline. One example of this is web surfing. You go from site to site without any thoughts about time.

Those who work through-time are extremely aware of the passage of time, so they make sure that they plan for things. For example, this type of person would choose their next free half-hour to browse through social media.

People who are a part of one or the other category could still lack some time management abilities. However, through-timers tend to streamline their activities and manage their time better by using a few helpful techniques. It is those who live their life in-time that need innovative ways to manage their time.

The first thing that people could do is to activate the attitude of self-reflection where you take some time to think about your thought process. When you do this, you will be able to change your thinking from, "I can, but…" to "I should," to "I must," to "I will."

The second thing that can be done is creating a motivational mechanism so that you will always be inspired to do the needed tasks in the hopes of getting something back.

While a lot of people think about motivating factors, more often than not, they tend to forget about them when they are distracted or tired. NLP tools have the ability to help create a better foundation for people to keep their motivation up. NLP teaches you to be single-minded and firm in your actions so that time-wasters and distractions will not interfere.

With this in mind, I want you to do something right quick. I want you to picture the two different futures that you could when you are 90-years-old; a negative one and a positive one.

The negative future is whatever the worse possible type of future could be. You don't have any money, friends, and your health sucks, you live on the street, and you get your meals in a food kitchen. This should be the future that scares you so much that you have a resounding "no" forming in your mind.

In your positive future, you have money, friends, health, happiness, comfort, and security. You look back at the things that you have accomplished with pride that you did the best you could. You squeezed every drop of juice out of every single moment. You saw obstacles as learning experiences so that you could make your life better for you and others. When you look back, you know that it was a life well lived.

Everybody needs a positive compelling or a negative compelling future. This is just a fancy way of saying that the thought of your future is either something that you want to stay away from or something that you want to happen.

Your future is yet to be decided. You have your own choices, and to a great degree, you are able to influence your future, but which future is going to be yours? Every single action, thought, and decision will lead you towards a positive or negative future. Which would you rather have? Until you are able to set a clear distinction between these futures and specifically map out the steps to achieve those goals, you might end up anywhere and this is what most people do.

In my own opinion, having an understanding of your own personality type, knowing the right people, money, and time are the most important resources. Given enough time and money, everybody could reach their goals, but time is limited. There is only so much time in the day.

You can gain knowledge, skills, experiences, understandings, possessions, and money, but time is the one resource that you can't control. Yet, time is the most valuable. Humans are great at wasting time. Let us count the ways:

1. Arguing with loved ones, family, and friends.

2. Mindlessly watching TV shows.

3. Aimlessly surfing the internet.

4. Wasting time on social media.

5. Traveling to work.

6. Not sleeping at night.

7. Negative thinking.

8. Surfing through junk email.

9. Handling telemarketers.

The best way to manage your time more effectively is to plan out your day in the morning or the night before and try to chunk activities into a manageable size. It also helps to stop and ask yourself questions during the day. Ask yourself what you want to be doing right now? What do I need to be doing? Things like that, to make sure that you stay on track with your goals.

To help you out with managing your time even more, here is an 18 minute time management plan.

Step 1: Set Daily Plan (5 minutes). Before you switch on your computer, grab a paper and pen and decide what is going to make your day successful. What will you be able to accomplish today that will further your goals? Write all of that down.

The most important thing here is to take out your calendar and schedule those tasks into your day. Make sure that you put the hardest task at the very beginning of the day so that you have the most energy to accomplish it. You need to decide when and where you are going to do something, otherwise, it should be removed from your list.

Step 2: Refocus (1 minute each hour). Set a timer on your watch or phone that goes off each hour. When you hear the ring, stop, take a deep breath, look at your to-do list, and see if you have spent the last hour productively. Then recommit to how you are going to spend the next hour.

Step 3: Review (5 minutes). Turn off your computer and review how your day has gone. What did you do well? Where did you lose focus? What distractions did you have?

This three-step process will help you begin and end your day on the right foot. Now, I do have one last thing for you about handling your time wisely. That is using a time management app. Todoist is on the top of the list for these types of apps. There is a free todoist or you can by $29 a year for premium todoist. The app allows you to assign your to-do list items due dates and you can sort them into different project labels. They also give you karma points when you consistently complete tasks.

There are other time management apps that can help improve your productivity as well, such as Be Focused Timer, Kiwake App, Focus Booster, and Loop – Habit Tracker. No matter what app you choose, stick with that one app. You will be amazed at how much better you manage your time.

Productivity Hack

The time has come for me to share the productivity hack that will change everything for you. This will involve creating a table of how you want your day to look and how important it is to take regular breaks.

When it comes to a daily schedule, there are two types of people:

- The minimalist who has a couple of recurring events, but a lot of free time for long periods of time.

- The overscheduler who creates calendars that look like finger painted pictures with overlapping meetings. They have their day planned out from the moment they get up.

These are both terrible for their own reasons. When you're overscheduled, you have no time for yourself. The more "in control" a person is over their calendar, the less control they feel that they have over their life. Plus, figuring out how long it is going to take to finish something is hard to estimate.

As for the minimalist, they are only living in la la land. They have likely offloaded all of their things in some way shape or form. Having a good daily schedule is the key to a successful life.

Start by creating time bookends for what is the most important work that you need to get done. Mark Twain once said that if the first thing you did in the morning was swallowed a frog, then the rest of the day would be a breeze. You want to create a time block for the most important things you need to get done.

What you don't want to do is begin your day with stress, emotional triggers, and distractions. Build recurring time into your day to accomplish what is most important before you do anything else. Your energy levels are naturally higher in the morning, and finishing something important will work like a domino effect that pushes you through your day.

Next, you can set up your complete schedule for the day instead of just the morning. This shouldn't look like the schedule of the overscheduler whose day is filled up with the priorities of others. Instead, you need to protect your time to do the things that you want to each day. This will give you the change to think about how you would like your ideal workday to look. If the way you have been spending your day isn't lining up, then you may need to re-evaluate your priorities.

Next, place your availability into the minimum amount you can, around ten to 15 minutes. With your meaningful morning and your skeleton schedule, the next thing you have to look at are the inevitable responsibilities, meetings, appointments, and tasks that will show up and screw up the day. A good schedule protects your time. So using processes that keep your time protected is a great place to start. Instead of setting meetings for 30 minutes or longer, set them for as short as possible. Try to aim for 10 to 15 minutes. Elon Musk has his day broken into five-minute chunks and the person requesting his time has to ask for more time if they need it.

Doing this, plus adding in intention open slots, will help you out for those last-minute surprises.

Next, you need to make sure that you are mindful of your flow. A good schedule will provide you with momentum and not take it away. People tend to forget their state of mind when they schedule tasks, meetings, or events. You don't want to make quick shifts from one task to the next. You need to schedule your activities in a way that flows naturally.

Next, you need to do a regular audit of your calendar to clear out dead time. Calendars aren't just for planning; they're also a great way to reflect. Every three months, take the time to look back at your schedule. Look at the time you spent on each of your projects, how you divided up your time, along with anything else that you can think of.

With all of this information, you can see if where you spent your time matches up with your intentions. If it's not, then you need to adjust your schedule.

Lastly, you have to make sure that you keep your commitments in a single place. You don't want to separate your personal and professional calendars. This will only cause troubles if you do because things are bound to overlap. Place everything on a single calendar so that you know the actual amount of time you have.

Now, you have learned how to make a good schedule, but there is another important part of this. You need to make sure that you have breaks. Have you ever been facing a problem that you couldn't figure out when you take a break, and then when you came back, you had figured out the solution? This shows the power of a break.

When you are working on something or thinking, your prefrontal cortex is at work and controls the thinking part of your brain. When you are working on goal-oriented work that you have to concentrate on, the PFC helps you to focus on your goals. PFC also controls willpower, executive functioning, and logical thinking. That's a lot of work for a little part of your brain. Here are some different ways and reasons to make sure that you take breaks during your day:

1. *Take a movement break.*

Constantly sitting places you at greater risk for developing obesity, depression, diabetes, and heart disease. Getting up every hour to take a walk or stretch will help your body and mind.

2. *You can prevent decision fatigue.*

Having to make frequent decisions during your day can wear down your reasoning and willpower. Decision fatigue can end up causing procrastination and simplistic decision-making. Try taking a 25-minute break whenever you can. This will give your brain some time to recharge.

3. *Breaks will bring back motivation for achieving your goals.*

When you have to focus on something with sustained attention, it can be fatiguing to our PFC. Taking your mind off of this can help to renew and strengthen your motivation to finish it.

4. *Take some time to connect with nature or with the city.*

Figure out if your mind needs to calm down or if it needs some excitement. If you need to calm down, then take a walk on a nature trail. If you are in need of some excitement walk, walk along the city streets to amp up your day.

5. *Switch up your environment.*

Briefly leaving your workspace and taking a walk somewhere else will allow you to switch gears and give your brain a break.

If you start to use everything you have learned about creating a schedule and making sure you take breaks, then you will be a productivity pro in no time.

Mistakes

While time management is very important, there are right and wrong ways to use it. Let's take a quick look at some of the most common mistakes people make when it comes to time management.

1. *Focusing your time on the wrong things.*

You should never let your goals slip to the wayside. Not working on the correct things is the main reason why people have trouble managing their time. In order to be productive, you have to know what you need to work on. For example, when things start getting crazy, they focus on the problem and start to blame others. The right thing for them to do is to focus on finding a solution.

2. *Trying to be perfect.*

Nobody is perfect, period. Let me repeat that again. Nobody is perfect. Don't worry about whether or not you can do it perfectly or even at all. Set your mind to what you want to do, and do it. Do it as well as you can. Don't focus on the little details right off. Start working, and those things will come.

3. *Not taking any breaks.*

I have a question for you. Do you believe that you are doing a lot of work or do you believe that you have too much time and not getting anything done? This is extremely subjective. A workaholic will likely feel that they don't have the time no matter the amount of work they put in. Somebody who isn't a workaholic may feel that they have done a lot need to rest. The point being is that you have to figure out the best balance between work and rest. You need to make sure that you take enough breaks so that you don't get burned out.

4. *Forgetting to create a to-do list.*

We've talked about the importance of to-do lists before. You have to create your to-do list so that you know what you need to do during the day. If you don't have a clear plan as to what you need to do, then you won't get anything accomplished.

5. *Getting a late start to your day.*

Most every successful person will start their days early. Howard Schultz, the man behind Starbucks, gets up at 4:30. Richard Branson gets up at 5:45. Tim Cook gets up at 4:30. When you get up early, you have time to jump-start your day and accomplish things that you normally don't get done.

Morning Routine (Make This a Habit for True Success)

Everybody is different. We all live different lives and we all have different goals. The one thing that we all need to do, though, is to plan out our day before it begins. The best thing you can do is to write out your to-do list for the next day. We're going to look at creating your morning routine to help you get your day started right.

It's tough being a morning person when you aren't one naturally. It takes a lot of discipline to get into the habit of waking up earlier. But creating a productive earlier morning routine could be what's standing between you and your goals. Think about these statements for a minute to see how many resonate with you:

- I went to be late, so I had to sleep later.

- I meant to get up early until the morning got here.

- I have too much going on at home in the morning and I don't have time for me, so why bother?

- I know what I need to do, but I don't have the willpower.

If you notice that you are nodding your head with these statements, then you're going to love this section.

What is the importance of creating a morning routine?

At the basic level, it will get rid of procrastination, be happier, healthier, and create success for your day. Think about this, how different would life be like if you were happier? The American Psychological Association performed a study that discovered following a morning routine would reduce your anxiety and depression. It causes your to-do list to seem less daunting.

But I hate mornings!

If you really hate mornings, the benefits may still now be swaying you in the direction of a morning routine. You may even be thinking that you hate them so much that there is no way that this could ever change. Guess what, you can do whatever you want. The key to creating a successful morning routine is your mind. You have to overcome the "I'm not a morning person" thought process. So if you continue to tell yourself that, your mind will make sure that it remains true.

Think back to the last time that you tried to get up earlier on a regular basis. To start, your motivation was probably high and you were ready to tackle everything. You went to bed earlier and set an alarm to wake you up at dawn. You were full of confidence for the next day. This probably worked for a couple of days.

However, the day came when the alarm hit off and you had no motivation. You hit the snooze button and stayed in bed because you were certain that today wasn't your day.

Don't worry, though, there is some good news. Motivation can become more permanent. There is no need to be motivated to do something because taking action will create motivation. There is a five-step process you can take to make sure you stick with your morning routine: reminder, routine, reward, rehearse, and record.

First, remind yourself of your morning routine.

Second, figure out the routine you want to do, meaning, what things you want to do during your morning routine.

Third, figure out the rewards that come along with your morning routine.

Fourth, rehearse successfully completing your habit.

Last, record your morning routine on your calendar once you finish it so that you watch yourself progress.

Alright, so the snooze button causes a lot of problems. If that is your first action when you hear the alarm, you are beginning the day with procrastination. You are telling your subconscious that you don't have enough self-discipline to even get out of the bed.

If you are one to pick up your phone and check social media and email first thing, you are placing other people's lives ahead of yours. You want to use your morning to focus on you. Hold off on checking your phone.

The key to making sure that you wake up in the next morning ready to kill the day is to make sure that you get a good night's sleep. Chances are, your mind is getting in the way of your sleep. Try a few of these things to silence your mind:

- Keep a journal and write out the things that stress you out to release them.

- Take a few minutes to practice some mindful breathing so that you can live in the present and not in the past or future.

- Quiet your inner voice and release it of any worries.

- Look back at the good things that you have experienced during your day, which will help your mind see everything that is right in your life while allowing you to release the little hiccups you may have experienced.

- Look forward to the great night's sleep that you are going to get.

The goals are to get your body ready for sleep, so make sure you don't eat a lot before bed or your digestive system is going to keep you up. Try to limit your alcohol intake. Too much may help you get to sleep, but the sleep won't be quality sleep. Plus, you may wake up with a hangover.

I know we're talking about morning routines, but having a bedtime routine may help you to get yourself ready for the next morning. It may be helpful to pick out the clothes you are going to wear the next day, that way it is one less thing that you have to think about. While you're at it, you can also grab your workout clothes as well.

Once you have everything together for your morning, you can do some fun things that will relax you. This could be listening to soothing music, taking a bath, or reading a book. You can do anything as long as it helps to calm you down. It could be tempting to use this time to go through your email or watch TV, but it is best if you can take the last hour before sleep to shut off electronic devices.

There are some things you can do to your environment to ensure you sleep well.

- Move your alarm so that you can't see the time. This will keep the glow and the time from keeping you awake. You may even want to place it on the other side of your room so that you have to get out of bed to shut it off in the morning.

- You could also make your bedroom a "device-free zone" and make sure all of your devices are in another space in your house. You could also just turn them off.

- Purchase a pet bed so that your pets won't bother you as much. (This tip is subjective to the pet. It doesn't work for all animals.)

- Try to keep the temperature of your bedroom around 65 degrees Fahrenheit. This is the ideal temp according to the National Sleep Foundation.

- Use blackout curtains to block out outside lights. This is especially important if there are street lights near your house or if you are located at the end of the road where you may have headlines shining through your windows.

Basically, you want to make your bedroom so soothing that it lulls you to sleep so that you wake up feeling great and rejuvenated.

Steps for Success

Now we're going to create you a morning routine. You can, of course, change this up a bit to suit you. You can also add things to it if you want.

1. *Hydrate*

The first thing you are going to do when you get up in the morning is to drink a glass of ice cold water. Of course, any other business you need to do before this you can, but the first action of your routine is drinking a glass of cold water.

This glass of water will help you to wake up, and the fact that it's cold will help even more. Whether you choose to drink cold water or room temp water doesn't matter, though. Drinking a glass of water first thing in the morning will improve your day no matter its temperature.

It helps to increase nutrient absorption by purifying the colon so that your body has an easier job of absorbing the important parts of food. Early morning water consumption will increase your daily blood and muscle cells. Water also boosts your metabolism, helps to moisturize and clear your skin, and balances out your lymph system.

2. *Breathing exercises*

After your glass of water, you're going to take some time to ground yourself through breathing exercises. Basically, you are going to take a few minutes to meditate and focus on the present moment and not the past or future. Performing breathing exercises each morning will reduce depression and anxiety, improve energy, increase relaxation, decrease stress, improve the immune system, and improve mental concentration.

This should only take you about five to ten minutes. It's a good idea before you start to blow your nose and to have tissues handy just in case you need them. Don't strain yourself and make sure you won't be distracted. If you start to feel anxious, stop the exercise. Lastly, begin slowly.

Here is an easy breathing exercise to try:

- Place a hand on your stomach and relax the abs muscles.

- Slowly breathe in through your nose and the bottoms of your lungs to fill with air. Your hand should move as your stomach rises.

- With this same inhale, feel the rib cage move out as the air starts to move up until your collar bones move.

- Hold the breath for a moment, and then breathe out through your mouth, gently releasing the air from the top all the way to the bottom of the lungs.

- At the end of the breath, pull your belly into your spine, pushing out all the air that is left inside.

3. *Exercise*

The next thing you will need to do is a workout. This can be any workout that you want to do. The important thing is to get your heart rate up for about 20 minutes.

While the important thing is just to make sure that you work out each day, doing so in the morning comes with its own added benefits. First off, you will end up consuming fewer calories. Brigham Young University discovered that morning exercise can make food less appealing.

It will set you up for more activity during the day. That means you will have more energy to accomplish the things that you need to. Your blood pressure will also be lower, by around 10%. When it comes around to night again, you will find that you sleep better. Evening exercises can leave your body too revved up for you to relax to get to sleep.

Cardio exercise is the best, so a good run, bike ride, swim, or even dancing are all great exercises to do first thing in the morning.

4. Visualize

The next step in your morning routine is visualization. You will take a few minutes to sit and visualize how you want your life to look. This practice will activate your subconscious mind so that you can generate creativity to achieve your goals. It will also help to program your brain so that it can recognize the resources that you need to reach your dreams.

This visualization doesn't have to be difficult. All you have to do is sit for a few moments and picture what you want your life to be. Be thorough when you do this. Think about every part of your life and what you would like to see.

5. Look at your goals

Once your visualization is done, you will look over your short and long-term goals. Take a look back at everything you have written down to refresh yourself. This will ensure that you know exactly what you need to be working towards.

6. Plan your day

Now, you will sit down and create your schedule for the day. You can either do a simple to-do list or create a full schedule. A schedule will help you be more accountable and may make your day easier. A schedule will show what you need to do at what time so that you don't feel overwhelmed by a list of to-dos.

7. Gratitude

The last thing you need to do before starting your day is to be grateful. During this time, you will write down things that you are thankful for. This will remind you of the good things in life so that you don't get caught up in the dwelling of the rough times. Be grateful for where you are currently and all of the opportunities you have. You are able to work through any task that you are presented with and you can reach every goal that you want to.

So many times, people start their days focused on the negative. Didn't get enough sleep. Not enough fruit for a smoothie. Favorite outfit is dirty. And the list goes on. This creates a bad day. You go around feeling like you're worthless and this leads to less productivity. Gratitude will help to pull you out of this problem.

Now, there are two ways you can do this. You can create a gratitude jar or write in a gratitude journal. Keeping either one of these brings about huge changes in your life. Practicing gratitude helps improve your sleep, keeps you from getting sick, and makes you happier.

For a gratitude journal, all you need to do is write down five things that you are grateful for. This can be anything and they only have to be a single sentence. But it's best if you take the time to really dig into the process. In order to make sure that you do experience the benefits of gratitude you have to:

- Don't just do it to do it. It works better if you go into this with the want to become happier and grateful.

- Try to go deep instead of listing out more. It's best to really explain the things you are grateful for instead of having a list of ten or more.

- It helps if you focus on the people who you are grateful for because it has a greater impact on you than things.

- Try subtraction. Instead of thinking about how things have helped your life, write about how your life would be without certain things.

- Write down things that were surprising or unexpected.

So, for a journal, you will write out some things that you are grateful for. If you want to create a jar, all you need is a jar and some scraps of paper. Write things you are grateful for on a piece of paper and put it into the jar. These are both great options, you can also look back over them any time you are feeling down. They can help to lift your spirits back up.

That's it for your morning routine. Do this every morning and you will notice that you have morning energy and you will get more things done.

The Truth about Productivity and Self-Esteem That No One Has Told You

Productivity and self-esteem work hand in hand. Both of these will come naturally the more you follow the steps that we have covered. Once you have reached a comfortable place with what you want in life and you start to create habits, then you will be set up for true confidence and happiness. But in case you're not positive about this happening, let's take a look at the relationship between productivity and self-esteem.

Have you met a person who has ever grown an oak tree from a pumpkin seed? Probably not, because the one thing that I am certain of is the law of nature, which is that you reap what you sow. Everybody is probably thinking, "Well, yeah." But the problem is that people don't really understand this because so many people try to get something for nothing.

No matter who you are, you would love to get everything you desire for free. People want more, but they don't want to put the effort into getting what they want. People don't understand value creation.

Value creation isn't you going to work at eight and going home at five. What you do between those times is what's important. For example, if you arrived late, ate breakfast at work, chatted with friends about what happened over the weekend, spent a few hours scrolling through Facebook, took a bunch of bathroom breaks, stayed at lunch longer than you were supposed to, and then shut down before the day was over, you would be subtracting value from your day.

There are studies who have found that most workers are only 50% productive at work. This is a waste of time. 35% of your life is typically spent at work. Think about this. How do you make more money? To make more money, you have to be productive.

Everything you do needs to be to the best of your abilities. Adding value to your work means that you find solutions to your problems, develop something new that you have always wanted to, and do things faster and accurately.

To know if you're adding value by being productive, write down five to ten successes you have reached by the end of the day. This will really show you how you are spending your time and put your life in perspective.

The main reason why people subtract value from their life is due to low self-esteem. Everybody views their self like a certain image, probably different than how others view them. This image you have about yourself impacts how you feel about yourself and how much value you place on yourself. Self-esteem can be changed though.

Looking for the positive, good, or learning experiences in things that you have done is a good place to start when it comes to improving your self-esteem. This is just another habit that you can create. People who are negative are more likely to have low self-esteem because they live on the bad things and the mistakes. They make their self feel useless even though they may have done a lot of good during the day.

When you start to realize that low self-esteem causes the majority of people's problems, you will start to see the issues of resistance to change, poor performance, and low productivity.

People who cultivate high self-esteem will succeed more in their personal and professional life. They are willing to put in the time and effort to reach their accomplishments. Let's dig a little deeper on this.

Whether you are working on your personal goals or working on a larger company goal, the only way you are going to achieve anything is to take action. This action needs to also be of quality and quantity. But, if you suffer from low self-esteem, you will sabotage your efforts without realizing it.

You've probably met people who are skilled and knowledgeable in their chosen field, yet their work always falls short of their potential. This happens because they don't believe in their self, or they believe in their abilities but they don't think they are worthy of success.

What's worse, is that people with low self-esteem don't think that they are worthy for great results so they will "dumb down" the things they do so that they don't stand out and won't get noticed. When you have a poor perception of your competency and abilities, you are setting yourself up to fail or reach mediocrity.

There is a strong relationship between lack of belief in worthiness and lack of belief in capability. Those who think they are competent but not worthy may end up being boastful. This ends up backfiring when their accomplishments don't match their claims. Resume padding is a common example of this problem.

Those who view their self as worthy but actually lack the competency will blame everybody else and everything else for their lack of results. They don't take responsibility. These people normally speak like they are self-important, but their results still don't back up their words. In both of these cases, people will quit trusting them.

We're going to take a look at an NLP technique that can help you to boost your self-esteem to make sure that you stay productive. But, I also want to remind you that your self-esteem and productivity will improve on their own if you follow the other things that we have covered as well.

It's a good idea to do this ten step exercise once or twice a day when you feel like you're struggling with low self-esteem. Doing this first thing in the morning is a good idea so that you can start your day on the right foot. Only through consistent practice will you be able to develop the habits that will improve your self-esteem when faced with everyday challenges.

1. *Imagine and relax*

Start by shutting your eyes and allow your body to relax. Take a few deep breaths. Now, take your attention to a person who you know genuinely loves and cares about you. Picture them in your mind and fully experience their radiance.

2. *Imagine you're writing*

Picture yourself at a desk in a magical room full of paintings and ornaments. You're sitting in a comfy chair with a pen in your hand and writing out your biography. You're writing out everything in your life and the way it has unfolded thus far. This includes the good and the bad. This story covers your past, present, and the unwritten future that you are fitting together.

As you write, you realize that the loving person you thought of earlier is standing on the other side of a glass door. They are observing you just like a guardian angel.

3. *Continue to write and feel*

As you look at that person, you start to write out some notes about their place in your story. You talk about their features, virtues, and qualities in detail. You also start to think about the amazing times the two of you have had together. You take a moment to think: How do I feel when around them? How do they make me feel about myself? How do they make me better?

As you think about these things, you experience a shock of confidence coursing through you, leaving you inspired and invigorated.

4. *Feel and Float*

You observe this person smiling at you. Their smile is warm and inviting and makes your heart happy. You are slowly drawn closer to them. In fact, part of you floats to stand with them. Both of you are standing there observing you write about your life.

5. *Look at yourself*

As you stand with your friend and watch yourself sit at the desk and write, you start to reflect on your thoughts and feelings. How do I look from this point of view? How do I feel about myself? What am I capable of achieving? What things could this person do in their life? You think about these things as you continue to watch yourself write.

6. *Become the loving person*

You turn toward the loving person. You take their hand with a smile and are pulled inside of them. You can see things now through their eyes, listen with their ears, and feel with their heart. You aren't you anymore. You are now a part of the loving person who loves you dearly.

7. *Change of perspective*

As you view yourself from this other person's perspective, you start to consider, think, and observe the way they see you. You ask: What do they think of me? How do they feel about me? What qualities do they see in me? What do they think I can achieve?

Don't question or judge the answers that come to mind. You stay mindful of these answers and you are filled with positive and warm energy coming from your loved one.

8. *Transfer their perspective*

Feeling as you do towards yourself, you start to detach your awareness away from the loving person. As you detach yourself, you move the emotions, perspective, and feelings that they have toward you back into your body sitting at the desk. As this happens, you will find yourself writing the feelings you are experiencing. You highlight the way that you feel and how it has changed your perspective about yourself and your world.

9. *Write the future*

You can now take the positive feelings and start to write out your future with a sense of appreciation. You ask yourself: How do I now feel about myself? What am I capable of? What kind of future can I create for myself? What fears can I overcome? What challenges can I tackle? How can I act with more confidence?

Reflect completely on each of these questions. You think about the impact that this is having on you and commit yourself to add positivity to everything that you do.

10. Awaken empowerment

As you finish up your story, the magical room begins to fade away. As it fades, you start to slowly return to the physical you. You are now back in the present. As you open your eyes, you feel positivity coursing through your body. You feel empowered. Everything seems possible. You ask: What's possible now? What can I achieve from this new perspective? What can I do to make my day extraordinary?

The answers you give these questions will help you to create the foundation for your life. Make sure that you remain consistent and don't ever give up with this practice and all the other practices that we have covered.

30-Day Challenge

We've made it to the end. Now the time has come for your 30-day challenge. Everything that I will ask you to do will help you with everything that we have talked about. Don't get frustrated if you feel like you aren't doing things right. As long as you do the best that you can, then you are doing it right. There are six things that I want you to do every morning, so make sure you take note and do them every day. Each day will have a separate action you will need to take. Your six daily actions are:

- Get up before 8 AM.

- First thing in the morning, do 50 pushups, 50 sit ups, and 50 squats.

- Take a cold shower. You take your shower like normal with the water warm and then shock yourself at the end with cold water.

- Perform one task that will help you reach your life goal.

- Do 20 minutes of exercising, preferably a session of running, bike ride, and skipping rope.

- Do not snack during the day.

Let's get started.

Day One

Today's special challenge is to commit. I want you to set a goal for what you want to accomplish during this 30-day challenge. You really need to challenge yourself so that you pull yourself out of your comfort zone. You can't choose to do something that you already do on a daily basis. You can also choose three bonus goals if you would like, but your main focus should be the first goal that is of the highest priority to you. Remember, your goal should be whatever you want. Maybe you want to write a book, so now you are going to actually sit down and write that book. You could want to learn how to cook a gourmet meal. Whatever it is, write it down and commit to reaching that goal in 30-days.

Day Two

Today you are going to declutter and organize. This can be physical clutter, work-desk spilling over with papers, computer filled with icons, or an inbox full of emails. To reach stress-free productivity, you need to declutter your environment. Clutter causes negative side effects to your focus and how you process information so get rid of it.

Day Three

Today you will focus and make things happen. You want to create a habit of working on your goals daily. The main reason why people don't accomplish things is that they let other stuff get in their way. I want you to schedule time for accomplishing your goals. Create an actual schedule and set reminders to make sure you don't forget to focus.

Day Four

Tonight I want you to take five to ten minutes to plan out what you are going to do tomorrow. As you sleep, your subconscious mind will work on the things you need to do. You will wake up the next morning having already figure out how to fix your problems.

Day Five

Today I want you to reward yourself. Sit down and think about different ways you could reward yourself for accomplishing things. Your rewards can be anything except for food item.

Day Six

Today you are going to review your productivity. Look back at the last five days and see what you have done well and what you can do better in the next week.

Day Seven

Today I want you to re-energize yourself by eating healthy. Pick foods that will help to cleanse your body as well.

Day Eight

Today you are going to schedule and prioritize the week ahead. Plan out the things that you want to accomplish in the coming week and create your reminders.

Day Nine

Today you are going to take action and get things done. Stop procrastinating and get to work.

Day Ten

Today you want to stay in the flow. Celebrate your success so that you feel happy for what you have accomplished, but keep a sense of urgency so that you continue to work towards your goals.

Day Eleven

Today I want you to work on self-discipline. You will find days where achieving your goals are easy and then there will be somewhere they aren't. You have to cultivate self-discipline to make it through the tough days.

Day Twelve

Today I want you to accept responsibility for your life. This means that you focus on the things that you can control and quit worrying about things that you can't.

Day Thirteen

Today you are going to solve problems. Problems are going to arise, but it's the way that you handle them that counts. Instead of focusing on the problem, look for the solution.

Day Fourteen

Today you are going to take some breaks. This doesn't mean you get the day off. You just get to add in some more time to recharge. This is something you should have been doing a bit of all along, but just in case, you now have permission to do so. Don't take too long of a break though, you don't want to lose momentum.

Day Fifteen

Today you are going to reassess things. The middle tends to be the trickiest part of all. To work through this slump, I want you to reassess your goals and remind yourself of the reason why you are doing this.

Day Sixteen

Today I want you to make sure that you are proactive with your happiness. It's important that you stay excited with what you do.

Day Seventeen

Today you are going to simplify by saying no. You have to say no sometimes to make sure that you achieve your goals. Being a yes man won't serve your best interests.

Day Eighteen

Today you are going to get rid of distractions. Turn off the TV, your phone, stop checking Facebook, or your email. Focus solely on what you need to get done.

Day Nineteen

Today you're not doing anything new, just make sure you stick to what you are supposed to do.

Day Twenty

Today I want you to think of your big picture and take small steps to get to it. It's a lot easy to write a couple hundred words in a day than 4000.

Day Twenty-One

Today I want you to look at your strengths. Look at what people praise you for and what you are most passionate about.

Day Twenty-Two

Today I want you to remind yourself that you don't need to be perfect. It's more important to do things than to be perfect.

Day Twenty-Three

Today I want you to switch up your environment. Do some of your tasks in a new place if you can. A change of scenery could provide you with new inspiration.

Day Twenty-Four

Today I want you to make sure that you remain motivated for this last week. Think about what would happen if you stopped and what would happen if you finished these 30-days. Which option would be better for you?

Day Twenty-Five

Today I want you to look at your energy levels. Figure out the times of the day where you have the most energy and adjust your tasks accordingly.

Day Twenty-Six

Today I want you to drink more water. Often people will forget to drink water and it is so important, so drink more water.

Day Twenty-Seven

Today is a day to focus on your tasks at hand. Go get things done.

Day Twenty-Eight

Today you are creating lasting habits. You have stuck to your goal for 28 days now, so you probably won't ever stop them.

Day Twenty-Nine

Today I want you to be grateful for how far you have come. Look back at the things that you have accomplished.

Day Thirty

Today, I want you to look over what you have done these last 30 days see how you have performed.

You've reached the end. I hope the challenge proved helpful and that you will stick with your new habits.

Conclusion

Thank you for making it through to the end of *NLP Productivity*, let's hope it was informative and able to provide you with all of the tools you need to achieve your goals whatever they may be.

You've learned a lot and it's okay if you feel a bit overwhelmed. The important thing is that you review what you have learned and start taking inspired action towards improving your life. Remember, the first thing you need to do is figure out exactly what you want in life. This means in your life, job, and family. You are living for yourself and nobody else, so make sure it's what you want and not what you think you should do.

With that in mind, you can start to use the NLP techniques that we have covered to improve your life ten-fold. Keep in mind that NLP is only part of the puzzle. You can also make changes to other areas of your life as well. Remember the foods that can help you increase your energy, as well as making sure that you get regular exercise.

You also have to make sure that you actually sit down and create your goals. Nothing is going to get done if you don't know what you need to do. Remember, don't let yourself get overwhelmed by your long-term goals, break them down into small and manageable pieces.

While learning all of this is fine and dandy, you still actually have to get started doing something. You have to create the self-discipline you need to achieve the things that you want in life. Create the habits that you know will help you in the long-term and stick to them. Don't let yourself fall back into bad habits.

None of this will get done if you don't start changing your time management skills. This is something that everybody struggles with. So many people will say, there are just not enough hours in the day, yet everybody has the same 24-hours. Those who know how to use those hours to their advantage are the ones who accomplish their dreams.

The fun part comes when you start putting all of these things together to create a new routine. As soon as you can, start implementing the morning routine that we covered. Make sure that you plan out your day so that you don't have any excuses. Also, get started on the 30-day challenge. It's fun and challenging, but it will help you to achieve everything that we have covered. The important thing is that you get started.

Finally, if you found this book useful in any way, a review on Amazon is always appreciated!

www.ingramcontent.com/pod-product-compliance
Lightning Source LLC
Chambersburg PA
CBHW072153020426
42334CB00018B/1989